Smiling Axes

Smiling Axes

Poems by

Lew Maltby

Cover design by Shay Culligan

ISBN: 978-1-949229-53-0

Kelsay Books
Aldrich Press
www.kelsaybooks.com

Acknowledgments

Grateful acknowledgment is made to the following journals, which published the poems below, some in a slightly different form, and to the North Dakota Poetry Society.

River Poet's Journal: "Dahomey Blues"

Stillwater Review: "Echo Company"

U.S. 1 Worksheets: "8th and Race, 5:30 a.m.," "Delta Visions," "Keeping the Faith," "The King Is Dead," "Om," "Woodcutters"

First prize in the North Dakota State Poetry Contest: "Hunting at Dawn"

Contents

Absalom

Child of fire.

Oblivious comet deaf to earth dwellers' fearful mumbling
blind to your frightening trajectory.

Tap dancer in a minefield,
beaming at passing shrapnel.

Golden pinball
in the asteroid machine.

We hold our breath
praying you don't tilt.

In The Bugaboos

Arise in darkness
force stubborn feet into complaining boots
and greet a frozen sun.
Climb above cozy forests
where aspen beckon with lacy fingers
and snowflakes dangle like poets'
shiny words in lazy air.
To higher ground, where mountains yawn
and push their granite cheekbones through the snow.
Where hungry winter prowls,
baring her yellow teeth upon the rocks,
ears straining for the careless tread of man.

Akureyri
81° North

Rain whispered on the roof
the day we rode the morning like a stallion
and folded the night sky into bed sheets
for our love,
bodies colliding like snowflakes
under the Northern Lights.

Lost

in the tangled forest of her hair,
I ate my trail of bread crumbs,
not wanting to be found.

Changes

She smiled and shook the dusty summer from her clothes,
set my timid winter skin on fire.

Brass mornings flew in that stallion season,
children stalked the heron's windy eye.

Then came the cedar voices of her green confusion
and the axe's rusty rhythm among the oaks.

Woodcutters

Chain saws cough
then snarl
and spit out frozen bark.

Chestnut-faced men with cinder voices
grip their sledges with angry knuckles
flash their smiling axes in the sun.

Joyful in their honest slaughter.

Hunting at Dawn

Sparrows explode like buckshot
as we stride across the farm's brown face,
free as foxes, mud-lucky in the clumsy dawn.

Hidden deep in cool-as-salamander thickets,
we watch crows wheel and fall like shaggy thunder from the sky,
catch the melting morning in cupped hands.

The King Is Dead

His portrait hangs in the lobby,
eyes following you in all directions.
He preferred the cartoon sketch on a grocery bag
from a cheap bar in Nogales, framed by a bullwhip.
The night he brought it home, we popped leaves
off backyard oaks until the neighbors called police.

The whip is silent now.
The portrait's eyes no longer move.
The cartoon hangs on the blistered wall of a grandson's
Roxbury walkup
beside an Amazonian blowgun for killing rats.

The one who taught me to fear nothing but himself
now cowers before the looming darkness,
while courtiers and jackals circle warily.

Who Knew?

Another stranger's face on a screen.

Another message in an electric bottle.

Another voyage across the Hudson,
  heart straining against the leash of in the moment.

Another trip to the plate,
  dirty spikes on a hitless streak.

Another best foot forward on worn sole.

Another night of uncertainty ending in wonder.

Who knew?

Keeping the Faith

With the ocean in your voice you called me.
We dove deep for shiny coins the masters scattered,
explored the windy corridors of logic,
and strained at the cranky armor of the law
many windmills ago.

Do you still bite into each new day like a fat red apple?
Are dogs of doubt yapping at your heels?
Does the wind still know your name?

Ocean

Sailor dreams of storms' fierce logic,
when in the fist of December seas.
Brother to the patient dolphin,
he listens to the night's round silence
wind rider of the cays.

Where the seahorse rides the iron swells
to greet the thunder's silky gong,
the bashful moon bends down to hear
the humpback whale's September song.

Toilers in the grouper's dismal garden
the sullen gull's harsh eloquence remember
join the ancient kelp dance in the sunken tavern,
and sleep within the nautilus' pink chamber.

El Tiburon
Roatan Reef

Tumbling through the looking glass
into Neptune's Coney Island
pastel coral rioting,
innocent trespasser betrayed only by bubbles.

Descending past clownfish's drunken staggering
in anemones' arms,
whirling blue galaxies of tang
and squadrons of barracuda

beyond where light turns back,
immune to my blue rapture,
on ambivalent quest.

El tiburon approaches,
intent opaque,
eyes black holes,
as indifferent as God.

Shadow Boxing

Flat rock skipping decades on a millpond,
　　now in dappled sunlight.

Etched memories dissolved into murky puddles.

Scarecrows waltz in a celebration of shadows.

Crooked roads converge, then splinter.

Dragons half slain.

`　　　　　　　Race half run.

　　　　　　　　Door half shut.

Dahomey Blues

Atchafalaya night,
red moon swimming in Chocolate Bayou.

Saxophone sings a runaway train,
switchblade rhythm slicing Cajun darkness
like a blacksnake through summer grass.

Echos of djembes and conch shells wresting
under jagged Dahomey stars.

Shark-dark eyes kneel on bloody earth,
waiting the benediction of the leopard's claw.

Delta Visions
Botswana

Okavango dawn,
buffalo roll, muddy river across a thirsty land.

Angry sun boils over the horizon
hammering the Kalahari like a dusty anvil,
mad dogs and Americans cower in the shade.

Black girls in white robes sing the darkness
where emerald embers of impala's eyes swim.

Acacias sway in thorny dreams
to hyenas' demonic lullaby.

Rolling Dice
Mount Pocono Raceway

Riding bullets of many colors
under the high priest's vigilant impassive eye,
we exercise faith with skeptic feet,
eating blue fear,
pass crippled fences
and gardens where twisted metal blooms—
monuments to miscalculation.

Going nowhere fast.

Echo Company
Fort Campbell, Tennessee

They took everything, even my hair,
and gave me strange new brothers.
We lie with our M-16s like lovers,
asleep inside the death machine.

Pieces of meat wrapped in green,
stuffed into trash bags if luck runs out.

My father thinks his son's a hero.
I do not correct him,
do not say I am only gazing
at a meteor shower of tracers
through barbed wire.

Serving Their Country

Last year's crop of spotless boys plowed under;
this year's patiently await their turn.

No Man's Land

Huddled in trenches, worried creases
on the land's dark brow,
waiting—bayonets erect—the command to advance
and engage in carnal combat
in no man's land,
where bodies hang like Christmas ornaments on barbed wire,
blood and semen mixing warily.

Unintended Consequences

GPA junkie at the learning factory
coddled and beer-fed as Kobe beef
bouncing on the trampoline to success.

Greek, impressionists, calculus
What are we studying for?
Don't ask me, I don't give a damn
Beats going to Viet Nam

They sprayed the fields in Mexico, man,
the weed's poisoned.

That's cool, just swallow this

Colors erupt
Boundaries dissolve
Sneak peek through the cosmic keyhole

Door ajar, mescaline, peyote, LSD, psilocybin,
methaqualone sneak in—
carousel of consciousness

Thank you, Richard Nixon

Beyond Fort Smith

Shy moon's fleeting glance.

Chiaroscuro shadow of the wolf pack.

Lonely sky dance of a red-tailed hawk.

Caribou thunderstorm rolling across tundra.

Wise geometry of Arctic char.

Strike a muffled chord in travelers' blood.

30th Street Station

Cold polished marble floors.
Grey anxious faces waiting.
A young child dances,

8th and Race
5 a.m.

Sun crawls like a crab across the sky,
smearing greasy light on warehouse windows—
wino badgers guard their doorway lairs.

Bulldozers sleep like dinosaurs in vacant lots
where scabby-kneed children sprout,
heedless to the shadow lessons of the street.

Cranes on rooftops, iron birds with ancient eyes, watch
hookers, sweet soldiers of the street, stagger home,
balanced on the jagged edge of morning,

The Shrug

Urgent, pointless questions disappear like water in the dust.
She would not speak the truth, even if she knew it.

The knot not cut, but slowly fraying
despite robotic assurances of canine loyalty.

The world ending in a shrug.

Her car door closes.
Tires spit gravel.
I do not hear.
I, too, am gone.

Om

Still as stone,
breathing,
seeking everything in nothing.

Ignore the mind, a stray dog wandering.

Sink softly
into the black hole—
the endless moment.

But I must feed the cat.

About the Author

Lew Maltby has an unusual background for a poet. He has been a factory worker, trial lawyer, truck driver, soldier, and corporate executive. He wrote his first poem at 35 in the wake of divorce. Urged by friends, he entered the North Dakota state poetry contest and was amazed when he won.

Lew finds the stuff of poetry in unlikely places—tracer bullets over his head in a minefield, the call of hyenas in the African night, the snarl of a chainsaw, prostitutes staggering home at 5 a.m.

His poems have appeared in *Stillwater Review, River Poet's Journal,* and *U.S.1 Worksheets.* This is his first chapbook.

LMaltby@workrights.org